About a Baby

Keith Edmonds

Cover Photo: Keith Edmonds and Wade Johnson

ISBN: 978-0-9910721-9-4

ISBN: 0991072197

Printed in the United States of America

KAM Publishing

DEDICATION

I dedicate this book to the victims of child abuse, in hopes of them becoming a Survivor of child abuse. The loneliness, the anger, and the confusion you feel are real; but to become a Survivor, you must find forgiveness for your abuser. I have learned that your feelings are always better "out" than "in." Find someone to talk to. Do NOT allow your feelings to take you down a path of self-destruction. You must dig within yourself to find forgiveness. Without forgiveness you are the only prisoner.

To my mother, I love you. What happened to me – to us – was a blessing from God. Our story started on September 9th, 1977, changed forever on November 18th, 1978, and is stronger today by the Grace of God. I hope you find comfort in knowing "the rest of the story."

Keith Edmonds

CONTENTS

ACKNOWLEDGMENTS

Special thanks to Wade Johnson for help with the cover design, as well as to Amanda Stearns-Pfeiffer and Elise Anderson for help with editing and formatting. To my family and friends for their unconditional love and support throughout this journey.

My name is Keith Edmonds. I am a grateful believer

in Jesus Christ, am a Survivor of child abuse, and

am also an alcoholic.

INTRODUCTION

And we know that in all things God works for the good of those who love Him, who have been called according to his purpose.

Romans 8:28 (NIV)

"Why would you want a picture of THAT?" It was at that time, four years old, sitting at a Kmart photo gallery in my best new clothes, smiling as brightly and as proudly as I could while getting my picture taken, that I realized I was different. My mother started crying and fighting with the girls who said those hateful words. I asked my mother what was wrong and why she was so mad. She collected herself and told me something that, for the first time, I would understand.

I have scars on my face from a mean man who tried to hurt me. As every other young child would, I had so many questions: Why would he want to hurt me? What did I do that was so wrong? She told me that I was going to be okay, that I could be anything that I wanted to be, and that he went away to prison for hurting me so badly. I said okay and continued to look out the window of our '81 Chevrolet Citation at the autumn leaves as we drove back to our home.

That would be the first time I realized I was different, and the first time I asked questions, but certainly not the last.

ABOUT THAT NIGHT

The night of November 18th, 1978, is a night that will play over and over again in my head each year that it comes around. A night that I wish I could have fought back, a night that I wish I could have changed, a night I wish I were not crying. It was as cold in my mother's apartment as the bitter Michigan winter weather.

The man that I was entrusted to – my mother's boyfriend, Michael Allen – had intended to change my life forever. That night I would become a victim and a Survivor of child abuse. Statistics show that most children who become victims of child abuse are 18 months old or younger: I was 14 months old. Statistics also show that most perpetrators are between the ages of 20 and 29: Allen was 25 years old.

The next morning, my mother awoke to find her baby boy swollen and clinging to life. She immediately asked my abuser what had happened. His reply was simple and calm: "I think it's a spider bite." After being rushed to the hospital and into the ER, the check-in nurse asked my mother what the problem was. My mother lifted the blanket that was protecting me from that same bitter cold and revealed the third-degree burns that I received on my face from this "spider bite." The nurse rushed me to a room where doctors immediately began to work on me.

My mother, not allowed to come with me, was taken to another room and separated from Allen, who was placed in yet another room. Questioning my mother and Allen's involvement, they asked how a child of 14 months could receive such traumatic burns to his face? This was no spider bite.

Doctors and surgeons believed the abuse I received was too much for an infant to handle and that I was going to die. Of the number of children who have died from abuse or neglect, 79.4% are younger than four years of age. That night I could have easily become a statistic at the hands of yet another violent crime against children.

As I lay there clinging to life, not having a full understanding of what life was, the doctors went out to my mother and told her to say her goodbyes to her son. It was at that point, for the first time, God's hand would pull me from the depths of death.

When they spoke to my mother about the accident that caused this burn, she claimed her innocence, knowing that she had nothing to do with harming her first and only child. My mother believes she was drugged and, still to this day, has no recollection of that night. Drugging her would have allowed this man to commit an inhumane act that nearly resulted in my death.

ABOUT THE ABUSE

The day after the abuse, my mother came to visit me at the hospital and tell me that my biological father was coming to visit me. The nurse questioned my mother. "His father has been in his room, holding him all night." My mother looked through the glass window into my room and her heart stopped: there I was cradled in the arms of my abuser. He was left with me, unattended, and was acting like he loved me. Was he there to show remorse? Was he there to cause more abuse? Was he there to kill me?

As it turns out, I had been tortured leading up to the near fatal abuse. I'd had cigarettes put out on the bottom of my feet. While it is still unclear as to who called Child Protective Services to my mother's apartment, it was determined that the cigarette burns on the bottom of my feet must have come from my babysitter who was a smoker.

It was a clever move on my abuser's part. Not a smoker, he was quickly dismissed as the offender. Once I arrived at the hospital, after the doctors had attended to the burns on my face, they also noticed that I had two broken legs. The cigarette burns were a warning shot from my abuser, not my babysitter.

ABOUT A MOTHER'S LOVE

The case worker that was assigned to my mother was Lois Firestein. She believed in my mother's innocence of the abuse right from the beginning, believed that she could win the custody case, and that my mother would never lose custody of me. However, my mother told Lois that she needed to stop fighting the custody case and that I needed to go into the foster care system.

She was a teenage mother, 19 years old, struggling with how to be an adult and a mom. Now she was dealing with the guilt of allowing herself to be involved with a man that nearly took her child's life. She knew that she needed to go get help, and she knew that she needed therapy to figure out why she was able to allow this to happen.

Lois asked my mother if she knew anyone in the foster care system. My mother's cousin, Kathy, was a foster parent. So, Lois went in front of the judge, asking that I be placed in care of Kathy and that my mother have full visitation rights, allowing her to come and visit me every day. The judge granted my mother this opportunity, and I became a ward of the State of Michigan.

It was the end of January 1979 – nearly three full months since I was abused – when I was released from the hospital. I walked out of the hospital with my mother holding one hand and my "Aunt Kathy" holding the other. My mother gave me a hug and a kiss, said that she loved me so much and that I was going to stay with Aunt Kathy for a little while, and said good-bye. I said good-bye and went with my Aunt Kathy to what would now be my temporary home.

While living with my Aunt Kathy, there was another foster child about my age named Bobby with whom I would play and have fun. It was a safe family environment for me, and my mother would come visit me every day. This gave her the opportunity to observe how my Aunt Kathy worked with the other foster children and learn parenting skills from these observations.

After six months of being a ward of the State of Michigan, the day before the custody court hearing, my Aunt Kathy came to my mother's apartment with adoption papers asking her to sign away the rights to her baby. My mother did not want to lose me and wanted me back. She wanted us to start a new life together and build a family.

When the custody court date arrived, it was late June. This was when my mother would find out if she would regain custody or not. She had made the difficult decision of placing me in foster care knowing that I deserved better. She knew she was broken, knew that she needed help. She was not afraid of the decision she'd made to temporarily give up her parental rights and had put her faith in God. She got the help that she needed, went to counseling for her emotional issues, and was able

to learn proper parenting skills from my Aunt

Kathy. With her faith in God, she listened to the

judge grant her full custody.

This time when we walked out of the

courthouse, she was holding me. I was reunited

with my mother and I was home.

ABOUT DECEIT

67th Judicial District Court

HONORABLE Donald R. Freeman,

Circuit Judge, at Flint, Michigan

After being extremely vague when my abuser talked in court about abusing me, and continually denying any intent to harm me, he finally agreed to go into detail about that night and the abuse. This would be the third time that the judge would see him. Each time he went in front of the court he would deny any intent of actually harming me.

Court records indicate I was held to a heat register because I was crying and had made a mess in my diaper. I continued crying. It was at the hands of that man, with intent to do great bodily harm, that changed my life forever.

Flint, Michigan, February 5th, 1979

The matter of People vs. Michael Allen, File Number 28749

Judge Freeman: *Mr. Allen, you can come up if you will, please.*

Judge Freeman: *Well, sir, how do you plead to the charge?*

Allen: *Guilty.*

Judge Freeman: *Tell me what happened, what you did and how you committed the crime, who was present?*

Allen: *I got up in the middle of the night and I, because he was crying, I told her he was crying. She said, "Don't worry about it, just go back to sleep he will just cry himself back to sleep." And it finally cried himself back to sleep and I finally turned off the TV, it was about one o'clock or so and I got up. I went to his bedroom. He had white stuff on his lips. I guess from the hot bottle that I gave him when he fell against the stove. And I wiped, I wiped his lips off, off his face.*

Judge Freeman: *You didn't intend to harm him?*

Allen: *Nobody harms.*

Judge Freeman: *I cannot accept a plea of guilt unless you admit to me that you intended to commit an assault upon this victim with the specific intent; Intent to Do Great Bodily Harm Less Than the Crime of Murder.*

> **Flint, Michigan, March 26th, 1979**
>
> **The matter of People vs. Michael Allen, File Number 28749**

Judge Freeman: *How sir, do you plead to the charge?*

Allen: *Guilty.*

Judge Freeman: *How old are you, Mr. Allen?*

Allen: *25.*

Judge Freeman: *In a strong, firm voice, tell me exactly what you did, who was with you, what happened, how you committed the crime.*

Allen: *I gave him a bottle of hot water.*

Judge Freeman: *How hot was the water?*

Allen: *To me it was just warm.*

Judge Freeman: *All right. Then what did you do that was wrong?*

Allen: *Well, his lips, later, my girlfriend put him in bed and I went in and checked on him because he was crying, and I told her he was crying, and she told me, "Don't worry about it, he will cry himself to sleep." And she went to sleep. And later on I went back in there, and he had white stuff on his lips, I* *wiped his lips off and…*

Judge Freeman: *His lips were worn off?*

Allen: *The lips and the side of his face.*

Judge Freeman: *His face peeled off, peeled off? You don't know what caused that, do you?*

Allen: *Not hot water.*

Judge Freeman: *But you didn't know that it would do that, that's what you just told me, didn't you?*

Allen: *Yes, sir.*

Judge Freeman: *You know, we've gone through this before, Mr. Allen, and I don't know why—I can't seem to impress upon you, nobody wants you to plead guilty if you are not guilty.*

Judge Freeman: *Now, from what you have told me is that you are innocent, is this right?*

Allen: *Yes, sir.*

Judge Freeman: *Well I can't accept a plea of guilt. You know that, because you have told me that you are not guilty of anything. You, see the point is this: If this is all simply an accident, if you didn't have the specific intent, it's not a crime, because it's the specific intent that makes up this crime, and they say you did something terrible. They said that you had intent to do great bodily harm against this one-and-a-half-year-old child, and that sounds pretty serious, doesn't it?*

ABOUT THE CONFESSION

Flint, Michigan, October 12th, 1979

The matter of People vs. Michael Allen,
File Number 28749

Judge Freeman: *Mr. Allen, you can come up if you will, please.*

Judge Freeman: *Now, I want to tell you something—and I don't spend time with people this way because we are just too busy—but this is about the third time you have been, walked through this courtroom, isn't it?*

Allen: *Yes, sir.*

Judge Freeman: *Did you tell me that you are pleading guilty to the charge of Assault with Intent to Do Great Bodily Harm Less Than the Crime of Murder?*

Allen: *Yes, sir.*

Judge Freeman: *Give me a time approximately.*

Allen: *I came home about one o'clock in the morning, me and her had been fighting and…*

Judge Freeman: *What did you then do?*

Allen: *Then I came in and I set the bags and stuff down in the living room so I could watch TV, and later on that night I heard the little guy crying.*

Allen: *And I heard him crying and I woke her up and*

told her to go and see what he was crying about.

And she said, "Don't worry about it, he will cry

himself back to sleep," and about half hour later he

went to sleep. And me and her had been arguing

for the last few weeks and, anyways she went to

sleep finally and I went in there...

Judge Freeman: *In Keith's bedroom?*

Allen: *He was in there alone.*

Allen: *She didn't put a blanket on him or nothing*

and I picked him up and he was wet and he started

crying again and he wet his pants. I changed him

and he had brownies all over him, and I took his

jumpsuit off and I went in the bathroom and, and

he started crying after I washed him off, and he

wouldn't quit crying and I just, I don't know, I hurt

him.

Judge Freeman: *What did you do to this 14-month-old?*

Allen: *I held him up against the heat register for less than a minute.*

Judge Freeman: *Why would you do that?*

Allen: *So he would shut up.*

Judge Freeman: *Did you, in fact, intend to do great bodily harm to that child?*

Allen: *At the time, yes, sir.*

Judge Freeman: *You intended to burn that child against that register, did you not?*

Allen: *Yes, sir.*

Judge Freeman: *All right, and did you achieve your goal?*

Allen: *Yes, sir.*

Allen: *I realized what I had done and I laid him on the floor and I put a wet washcloth on his face and, I don't know, his lips started peeling and, or they had a little, I don't know, skin, I guess, and I wiped his face and the skin came off onto the washcloth, and then I put baby oil on his face and took him to the hospital.*

Judge Freeman: *You were just a little peeved because a 14-month-old child was crying?*

Allen: *Yes, sir.*

Judge Freeman: *Incidentally, did your burning his*

face stop his crying?

Allen: *No, no, and I held him until he went to sleep, and he stopped.*

Allen: *I'm guilty.*

Judge Freeman: *All right, then, sir, I do accept your plea of guilt.*

ABOUT HIS SENTENCE

> Flint, Michigan, November 15th, 1979
>
> The matter of People vs. Michael Allen, File Number 28749

Judge Freeman: *The sentence of the Court is that you be confined to the State Prison at Jackson for not less that eighty (80) months and not more than ten (10) years. I direct the Department of Corrections to make certain that you are never placed on a trustee duty, that you are never placed in a residential center, that you are never placed in a circumstance where you can inflict harm upon* *children again or be available to move around in the court system where it is possible that you could come back and seek retribution against the mother of the victim of perhaps that poor child again. It's my thought that you should remain behind prison walls at Jackson Prison until you serve every single day of that sentence and let your conscience guide you.*

"Mr. Allen, I'm not ordinarily touched and affected by ordinary criminal behavior. We live in a violent society. We live in a society where people seem to have somewhat less of a standard of morality than I would hope they would, and I see many offenses that are committed against others. And although each one is heart rendering, you know, there is something very, very pathetic about a circumstance where a child, a beautiful, beautiful boy, fourteen-months of age, has his face put up to an electric wall heater, causing second and third-degree burns, leaving this child the rest of his life looking like that, like a raw piece of meat; he doesn't know the gruesome features that he is about to face because of this vile, inhumane act that you committed on him. And I look at this *child's record and I'm not saying that you are responsible for it but, here's a child who had two broken legs, I don't know how that could happen and you are not blamed for it. Here's a child with cigarette burns over its body and I think, 'What more could have ever happened to a sweet, innocent being?'*

Now there is a God up in Heaven. I hope he looks at you and wonders, 'What makes this possible?' I see a child screaming through the night, pleading for help, with these burns all over his face, and being ignored. I see the skin peeling from its face. I don't know how you could treat a human being that way, if you had a fiber of decency in you. You must be totally devoid, without feeling for others. You must be cold, indifferent, uncaring. I've seen criminals who do evil things to adults, and I have more respect for them. They have a chance to protect themselves. What was that fourteen-month-old little child going to do when its face was scalded on an electric wall heater?

And I remember the times that you came into court and said it was all a terrible accident. But when the time finally came for you to recite what you did, in your own handwriting you said this: 'He kept on crying. I went into a rage. I held him up to the heater in the bathroom for less than minute, and I realized what I was doing and I lay him on the floor in the bathroom and I took a wet washcloth, put it on his face until he stopped crying. And then I took the washcloth off the little guy's face, I noticed his skin was peeling around his lips. I wiped his lips and the skin stuck to the washcloth. Then Brenda

woke up.'

And I will tell you this: that I called Child

Protective Services today and I asked them, also, to

make a further investigation as to whether the

mother of this child was present while this was

going on and is the person who should have that

human being entrusted to her, and I'm going to ask

them to review her position with respect to that.

Well I only hope that in prison, where I'm told

that in that society there are various qualities of

criminals and they have their own caste system so

that somebody who commits certain types of

crimes is considered to be - for lack of better

expression—a better criminal because he is

involved in a certain degree of talent of

wrongdoing- when they come down to the bottom

of the heap and they say, 'What crime did you

commit to get here?' That you say, 'I took a

fourteen-month-old baby boy's face and pushed it

against an electric wall heater and burned him for

life.' Then you'll probably receive the type of

consideration that even criminals give to each

other. I hope you never forget it. I only wish it were

scarred on your face as it was scarred on that

child's face."

— Judge Freeman

ABOUT MY SENTENCE

My abuser received ten years in a state prison for being found guilty of the Intent to do Great Bodily Harm Less than the Crime of Murder to a child, and I received a life sentence of feeling alone, alienated, and angry.

There were often times as a child growing up a Survivor of child abuse, that I would ask myself those same questions that I asked my mother at a very early age. Why did he want to hurt me? What did I do that was so wrong? As a child growing up, I always felt alone. In my own solidarity, my mind always went back to those same questions. That is where my loneliness began, my confusion grew and my anger built.

ABOUT THE BURN INSTITUTE

Each year until I was 14, then every-other year after I turned 14, my mother and I, and sometimes family members who would want to travel with us, would drive to the Shriners Burn Institute in Cincinnati, Ohio. I would continually look out the window watching the trees turn to city lights and wonder why *I* have to go receive check-ups. Why did he want to hurt me so bad? What did I do that was so wrong?

This was my least favorite place on earth. When I was there, I was angry. I would have to have multiple photos taken of my scars; they wanted photos from every angle, and they wanted me to smile while they took what felt like thousands of photos. Why would I want to smile? I've never enjoyed being a subject of pictures – when you have scars on your face as a child, one of the last things you want is someone taking photos of you. When I look at photos of myself, all I see is the damage from my abuser. I was expected to live a "normal" life with a constant reminder that I was abused for crying as an infant.

Once they finished taking all the photos, I would have to go into a cold white room and wait, just me and my mother sitting in a room until the doctors arrived. I would tell her how much I hated it there, and that I didn't want to be there. They would come in the room and discuss the pictures right in front of me with their deep dark tones. The words that I heard were: "Ohhh, look at that," "Ouch," "Poor kid." While those weren't the exact words they used, those were the words that I heard and felt.

My surgeon was an older gentleman with dark black hair; he wore glasses that fit on the tip of his nose, almost like he was looking down on me. The room was always well lit but there was a sense of tension, tension that could be matched to an interrogation room in a jail. He would touch and stretch my scar, talk into a little recorder box, and document everything that he saw. Then, he would recommend me a fitting for another mask.

The doctor who was in charge of creating the mask was a short stocky guy, light brown hair and did nothing but remind me of Pat Sajak from *Wheel of Fortune*. To this day, I cannot watch that show without him running through my mind and hearing him say, "You have to stay still or we are going to have to hold you down," while I was screaming and crying because I was against having to wear a mask. I had already been abused and had scars on my face: I was already different. Why would I want to wear a mask that was painful and more degrading? I would have to lie flat in a cold room while they layered on paste that would form to my face, cutting out holes for my eyes, nose, and mouth. It felt like I was being buried alive. The whole time I was kicking and screaming in anger and rage. Why do I have to go through this? What did I do that was so wrong? Why did he want to hurt me so badly?

Each and every year as I grew, I would have to go through the same emotions and procedures to get fitted for a new mask. Each year I built up more and more hate for my abuser. I would have to say the doctor that created my mask was by far my least favorite person at the burn institute. The mask would make me look even more different, having it stuck to my face, pulling and stretching my scar.

This would prove to be a constant battle when we got home from my yearly check-up. My mother would try and force me to wear to the mask, and I would continue to fight to not wear it. I was

supposed to wear this mask all day, just taking it

off enough to allow my skin to breathe. I would

only wear it for a little bit in the evening, then I

would take it off once she closed the door to put

me to bed.

ABOUT LETTING GO

In the fall of 1987, I was ten years old and entering the 4th grade. However, this year I was not starting the school year on time.

I was getting ready for the first surgery that I would remember. I went to have my nostrils enlarged. After I was abused, my nostrils shrunk from the burns and it was causing troubles breathing. They took skin from behind my ears, placing two catheters in my nostrils and allowing the skin to build up around them. Two months later, the catheters were removed.

When I was 12 years old, I started to understand that my mother and the surgeons were discussing the option of doing more surgeries – surgeries that would allow them to completely reconstruct my face. It was at that point that my mother and I had a discussion about whether these surgeries were going to take place. I told her that I did not want any more surgeries, even though it could mean that my scars would be less noticeable. I was ready for the mask, the surgeries, and the trips to be over.

With that, I started to grow into the man that I am today. I accepted the fact that I am a Survivor of child abuse, and I would face this world without feeling shame or guilt for being abused.

Wearing the mask became less of an issue, the surgeries finally ended, and the trips to the burn institute were few and far between. It was at this time that I could finally focus on trying to be a "normal" kid, which led to me becoming a "normal" adult.

ABOUT FORGIVENESS

There comes a time when you take a look at someone who has wronged you. Whether they bullied you, told lies about you, stole something from you, or abused you, you ask yourself these questions: Why did this happen to me? What did I do to deserve this pain?

Your initial thought is revenge: "Well, I am going to get even with that person." Then you think about resentment: "I HATE that person. I cannot stand that person. How could they do that to me?"

There is a secret to living a life that you love,

that you enjoy, and that you look forward to living each and every day. That secret comes from *forgiveness*.

It is as simple as saying to yourself that you forgive the person that wronged you. I have lived a life filled with ridicule, anger, and hate. I was tortured and abused as a child. I lived through the torment of other kids making fun of the way I look. I have lived through, and still do today, the stares while out in public and I have lived through discriminating situations.

There were times when I would come home from school each day, go into my room where I was alone, and I would cry, I would scream. I did not understand why I had to go through what I was going through. But no matter how many times I thought of Michael Allen, I asked myself, "Does he care that I have this scar? Does he care about me?" Each time, I would come up with the same answer: No.

This realization led me toward anger and acting out. But one day, one fine day, I came to another realization. If I held on to this anger – this hate – the only person that I was harming was myself. You see, when you are holding that grudge or plotting that revenge you are only holding yourself back.

There are very few promises that I can give you. But the one that I have is that if you let go of things from the past that have hurt you and *you* find forgiveness, it will set you free.

It took me a very long time to find forgiveness for the man that so violently changed my life . But I was able to find it at a young age after asking myself over and over again if he cared about what he did to me. I was not going to let myself be a prisoner of this man, and I was going to live a life that I love and cherish.

It has been through the grace of God that I have been able to live this life without seeking revenge and without carrying resentment or hate towards this man. I know that God was with me that bitter cold Michigan November night, and I know He is with me today.

I did eventually find forgiveness for the man

who tortured me, nearly killed me, and changed my life forever. I was also able to find forgiveness toward my mother for allowing me to be put in a situation that resulted in my life, our life, being changed forever.

It has been 12,827 days to the day I write this, and I have never heard "I am sorry" from my abuser. You can wait a lifetime to hear those words and may never hear them. Should that dictate your happiness? Forgiveness does not change the outcome of a situation, forgiveness does not excuse a person for their actions, but forgiveness does allow you to build a life that you love.

I am proof, I persevere.

My name is Keith Edmonds. I am a grateful believer

in Jesus Christ, am a Survivor of child abuse, and

am also an alcoholic.

ABOUT THE AUTHOR

Born and raised in Flushing, Michigan, Keith

Edmonds graduated from Central Michigan

University with a Bachelors of Applied Arts degree

in 2002. After spending a short time in Omaha,

Nebraska, he moved to Nashville, Tennessee in

2010. He speaks throughout the country on behalf

of child abuse victims and Survivors.